Favorite
CLASSIC
Melodies

T0069330

VIOLIN

Arranged and Recorded by David Pearl
("Brandenburg Concerto No. 5, First Movement" arranged and recorded by Donald Sosin)

Cherry Lane Music Company
Director of Publications/Project Supervisor: Mark Phillips

ISBN: 978-1-60378-414-6

Visit our website at www.cherrylaneprint.com

CONTENTS

AVE MARIA

VIOLIN

By Charles Gounod and Johann Sebastian Bach

BRANDENBURG CONCERTO NO. 5, FIRST MOVEMENT

By Johann Sebastian Bach

VIOLIN

CARO MIO BEN

VIOLIN

By Giuseppe Giordani

Errata
This page replaces page 6.

TRACK 3

CARO MIO BEN

VIOLIN

By Giuseppe Giordani

Moderately slow

Orchestra

CLAIR DE LUNE

VIOLIN

By Claude Debussy

FUNERAL MARCH OF A MARIONETTE

VIOLIN

by Charles Gounod

Moderately fast, in 2

9

GYMNOPÉDIE NO. 1

VIOLIN

By Erik Satie

HALLELUJAH CHORUS

from *Messiah*

VIOLIN

By George Frideric Handel

HUNGARIAN DANCE NO. 5

VIOLIN

By Johannes Brahms

Moderately

Slower

Tempo I

MINUET
(from String Quintet in E Major)

By Luigi Boccherini

VIOLIN

Moderately

PIANO SONATA NO. 14 "MOONLIGHT"
First Movement

VIOLIN

By Ludwig van Beethoven

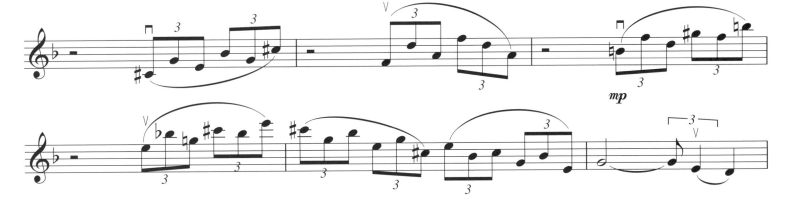

15

SYMPHONY NO. 5

First Movement

By Ludwig van Beethoven

VIOLIN

Moderately fast

Orchestra

WILLIAM TELL OVERTURE

VIOLIN

By Gioacchino Rossini

Moderately fast

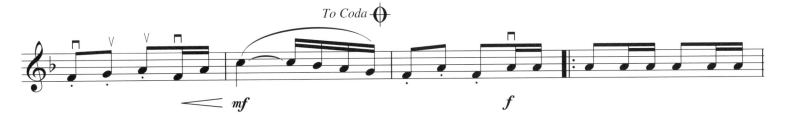

POMP AND CIRCUMSTANCE

VIOLIN

By Edward Elgar